Dungene

Chris Thom

T0249278

methuen | drama

LONDON · NEW YORK · OXFORD · NEW DELHI · SYDNEY

METHUEN DRAMA
Bloomsbury Publishing Plc
50 Bedford Square, London, WC1B 3DP, UK
1385 Broadway, New York, NY 10018, USA

BLOOMSBURY, METHUEN DRAMA and the Methuen Drama logo are
trademarks of Bloomsbury Publishing Plc

First published in Great Britain by Methuen Drama 2018
Published in *National Theatre Connections 2020* by Methuen Drama 2020
This edition published 2020

Cover design: Ben Anslow
Cover image: Dulcie Peek-Pullum at Dungeness (2018)
(Photography © Emily Balham / Store Room Youth Theatre)

A catalogue record for this book is available from the British Library.

A catalog record for this book is available from the Library of Congress.

ISBN: PB: 978-1-3501-9477-9
ePDF: 978-1-3501-9478-6
eBook: 978-1-3501-9479-3

Series: Plays for Young People

Typeset by Mark Heslington Ltd, Scarborough, North Yorkshire

To find out more about our authors and books visit
www.bloomsbury.com and sign up for our newsletters.

Welcome

I don't know where you are right now, or when you're reading this. But wherever you are in the world, I welcome you to the Dungeness community. We're happy to have you.

The first person I ever told I was gay was my friend Eve. She was in my year at school. We were crossing the road near Charing Cross station and as I said the words *I'm gay* I could feel myself collapsing. Eve held me up and got me to the other side of the road. Suddenly everything felt different. Like all my life until that point had been blurry, and now everything was sharp and in focus.

I would love the next sentence to be: 'And I never looked back.' But that would be a lie. I didn't believe in God and yet I lost count of the times I prayed for me not to be gay. I was bullied for being gay before I came out and I was bullied for it after. But in that moment, in Eve's arms, I was safe.

Looking back now, I realise that for much of my life I believed I was disgusting. It's what I was told. People said it in a variety of ways. Sometimes through violence, other times more subtly. But I took it as an indisputable fact.

The first time I was beaten up for being gay, I was eighteen. A group of boys who looked much younger than me attacked me on a train. They had an iron rod and knuckle-dusters. The resounding memory I have is screaming at other passengers for help. But people just stood and watched. Now I understand that they must have been scared too, but it took me a long time to forgive them. I was able to forgive my attackers far quicker than I could the bystanders.

I needed hospital treatment, but I didn't go. I was too humiliated that kids who were younger than me had beaten me up. But more than that, I was too ashamed to tell people that they were screaming the word *faggot* in my face as they attacked. It never even occurred to me to tell the police. I had no faith in them whatsoever to protect queer people.

But it wasn't just this violence that brought about my self-loathing. It occurs to me that every law passed against LGBT+ people, including Section 28, came from a place of disgust. The media attacked LGBT+ people. In school we were erased. And I absorbed it like a sponge. If you had squeezed me I would have drenched the floor with shame.

I am telling you this because, despite many friends and family who were supportive, I felt alone.

And I want you to know that you are not alone. If you are reading this book, you are not alone.

Imagine each copy of this play is like a beacon on top of a lighthouse. It sends out a signal, into the night, and connects you with everyone else who has ever read or performed this play. They could be sat right next to you; they could be in a country far away. You are not alone.

When I was at school I self-harmed. And although eventually I stopped cutting into my legs with scissors, in my early twenties I starting self-harming in different ways. At the time I thought I was having fun – but the endless nights of partying, substance misuse and my fear of intimacy were all just ways to achieve the goals of numbing the pain and hiding from this truth: somewhere along the line I had learned to hate myself.

I thought I was ugly. And the most natural, biological feeling – for me, being attracted to another man – filled me with shame. But if you had told me that, I'd have told you to piss off.

We talk so much about learning to love ourselves it has almost become clichéd.

But the fact of the matter is many LGBT+ people have been deeply wounded.

To heal our wounds is to let go of shame.

To turn your back on shame is to make a commitment to yourself.

It's a life-long commitment.

And we need to be clear that the cause of the problem doesn't lie with you. It lies with others.

For a long time I thought falling in love would heal me. I'd meet a man and he would love me and all my shame would melt away. I did meet men. And they did love me. And I loved them. But I still hated myself.

The big change came when I decided to stop asking other people to heal my wounds. These wounds weren't my fault. But I had to heal them myself.

And the first step, for me, was when I stopped denying myself my own love and respect. All the love I wanted from other people, I decided to give to myself.

Little by little, I began to like myself more. I began to unlearn all the bad stuff I'd been told about myself. And slowly I stepped out from the shadows of shame, and walked in the sun.

I definitely still have some steps to take on this journey of self-love. But when I think back to where I started, it's a journey I'm glad to be on – loudly, proudly, and with no apology.

And wherever you are on your journey, no matter your starting point, I want you to know that you are wonderful and brilliant.

If you're in a place where people don't accept you, or you don't accept yourself right now, please know that there are people out there who will love you unconditionally.

But any steps you can take – even small ones – towards giving *yourself* that unconditional love, are steps worth taking.

You'll never look back.

Chris Thompson

Playwright Chris Thompson speaks to director Audrey Sheffield about the opportunities and challenges when staging the play.

If you had to summarise in one sentence what this play is about for you, what would you say?

This is the play I wish I'd seen when I was growing up.

What is the significance of the location of the play?

Dungeness is my favourite place in England. It sits on the edge of the country, and although it looks barren, it is secretly teeming with life. It's a resilient, unapologetic place. When you go you there, you feel windswept and exhilarated, which is what love can feel like sometimes.

What are the most important themes you'd like companies to explore and draw out in their rehearsals and productions?

Commemoration, protest, self-acceptance, forgiveness, love.

Do you have any tips or ideas to help directors work around potentially personal or challenging themes (i.e. faith, culture, sexuality and bullying) that are raised in the play?

There is definitely a duty of care to your actors and audience in this play. I believe that asking young people to participate in *debates* around their identity is abusive. The right of LGBT+ people to exist is not a point for debate. It should be treated as a given.

If actors choose to bring their own experience into the rehearsal room, a robust confidentiality agreement should be in place. There is no expectation anyone discloses anything about their sexuality or gender identity to be able take part in this play.

If people choose to reveal aspects of their identity, it is to be celebrated! I've had loads of messages from young people, parents and teachers saying that the play provided a catalyst for some wonderful coming out stories and a springboard for beautiful and accepting conversations.

We just need to be mindful that LGBT+ young people might find elements of the play close to home, and to make sure there is a nurturing and supportive atmosphere so everyone feels held and safe. The same goes for your audience.

And you might find you've got some out and proud kids ready to shout it from the rooftop and this play gives them the loudspeaker. That's wonderful too. The message is: come as you are.

What if the company doesn't have a choir? What might be some staging options for the final scene?

I've seen successful versions without a choir. You could make the audience the pride march. Just keep it punchy – be bright, be brief, be gone.

Do you have any tips or suggestions on how to help maintain momentum and engagement when the entire play is essentially one long scene – set within one space and in real time?

Pacing is a real challenge. The whole play is set against a countdown towards a specific moment, so in the most part you need to ensure each beat is driving the story forward to this event. If you look at structure you'll find there's several smaller climaxes in the play and it ebbs and flows between smaller, intimate moments and bigger group moments. I'd find these smaller arcs within the play's overriding main arc and break the play into logical segments. Even in the quieter moments, ensure every moment is about character and story.

I've given several characters monologues. When I was writing I thought of them as arias in an opera – self-contained, for one voice. Don't be afraid to give these moments space, but it's important you find the pace again when you come out of each one.

When it comes to the two-minute silence, don't be afraid to break the fourth wall. Every performance of this play is both a protest and an act of commemoration.

What flexibility is there around casting (re: gender, ethnicity, sexuality)?

The characters can be played by actors of any ethnicity. In terms of sexuality, you don't need to be LGBT+ to be in this play: performing it is a way of being an activist and an ally.

Can you give three important things or thoughts about this play for directors to re-visit if ever they feel wobbly at any point through this process?

1. Don't overthink it. The play doesn't need directorial bells and whistles. Focus on character and story. Keep it truthful.

2. Put yourself in the position of the audience. What are you making them watch *right now*?

3. Don't be afraid of the joy and absurd humour. The play is sincere but it has a twinkle in its eye. Treat the characters and themes with respect and dignity but don't make your production too worthy.

If you were backstage with the company just before their first performance, what would you say to them?

Be generous and supportive to your castmates, and if you're enjoying yourselves, your audience will be with you every step of the way. Loud, proud, and no apology.

www.christhompsonwriter.com

www.audreysheffield.co.uk

Foreword

I was completely overwhelmed when I saw *Dungeness* being performed at the National Theatre in London and knew immediately that this play told a story that so many LGBTQ+ people could resonate with. The journey of self-discovery, layered with the anguish of being rejected by the people who are supposed to love you the most, comes across beautifully. I cried with joy to see the young people on stage step briefly into their authentic selves to celebrate Pride.

I am overwhelmed again, this time with gratitude, to Chris and Methuen Drama for their kind donation to Stonewall Housing. By buying and studying this play you are supporting thousands of young people like Jotham, Franny and Orson and, on their behalf, I want to say thank you.

We will do everything we can to make sure that all LGBTQ+ in the UK always have somewhere safe to call home.

Together, we will end LGBTQ+ homelessness.

Steven McIntyre
CEO Stonewall Housing

stonewall
housing

Stonewall Housing is a charity in the UK working with Lesbian, Gay, Bisexual, Transgender and Queer (LGBTQ+) people who are homeless or at risk of homelessness.

We were founded in 1983 by a small group of women who were concerned that housing providers were disregarding the needs of lesbians and gay men. Even though many years have passed and we have legislation protection LGBTQ+ rights, we are still very concerned about this now. LGBTQ+ people continue to be over-represented in homelessness services which means we still have a lot of work to do.

We help LGBTQ+ people to find somewhere safe to live. People get in touch with us every day telling us they have nowhere to go and don't know what to do. We help them understand their rights and provide step-by-step instructions so they can get the right support from the right people. We also help LGBTQ+ people who have found somewhere to live temporarily and support them to get settled in and get ready to live independently in their permanent home.

Our mission is to end LGBTQ+ homelessness.

You can access more information and LGBTQ+ lesson plans as well as ideas on how you can support Stonewall Housing at www.stonewallhousing.org/education

Twitter @stonewallhousin
Instagram @stonewallhousing
Facebook www.facebook.com/stonewallhousing

Supporting Stonewall Housing

If you would like to join the fight against LGBTQ+ homelessness, we want to hear from you.

You can support us by helping to spread the word: like and follow our posts on social media and write your own posts about LGBTQ+ homelessness, tagging us.

You can make a regular or one-off donation or even host a fundraiser with your friends, at school or at work. You could host a quiz, have a cake sale or arrange to jump out of a plane, all in aid of Stonewall Housing.

You can remember Stonewall Housing with a gift in your will and help future generations of LGBTQ+ people to live in safe homes.

We have loads of ideas and would be very happy to talk them through with us. Please do get in touch at fundraising@stonewallhousing.org

Acknowledgements

My thanks to:

Tom Lyons.

National Theatre Connections.

Audrey Sheffield.

Steven McIntyre and Stonewall Housing.

Dom O'Hanlon and Methuen Drama.

All the *Dungeness* companies so far . . . and those to come.

Dungeness

Characters

Birdie
Orson
Jotham
Jen
Adira
Franny
Tana
Caia

Setting

New Romney town centre. Not far from Dungeness beach.

The communal room of a semi-independent home for young people. It's a large house that has been converted for communal living for young people. It's a strange mix between attempted homeliness and doctor's waiting room. All the doors are fire doors, and there are emergency fire exit signs and a fire blanket. It feels like there's been a risk assessment on every bit of furniture because there probably has. The TV is locked in a cupboard. There are beanbags and a sofa and arm chairs and the stained carpet looks like it's from a school staff room. The room has been painted bright and happy colours by previous residents, which makes it all the more depressing.

The window is frosted so the light comes in but you can't see in or out. The same window is cracked from where someone has thrown a stone at it from the outside.

Somewhere on the walls are the house ground rules and a wall display which are referred to later in the play. Also on the wall are the Stonewall posters, which say, 'Some people are gay/trans/bi etc. Get over it.' And next to them is a washing-up rota.

Text

/ means the following speaker overlaps.

– means a character deliberately remaining silent or struggling to find the words.

They've just started a house meeting. Everyone is there except **Caia**.

Birdie   I say BOOM.

Silence.

I say BOOM.

Silence.

I say BOOM-CHICKA.

Silence.

I say BOOM-CHICKA-ROCKA-BOOM.

I say BOOM-CHICKA-ROCKA-BOOM.

Jen?

BOOM-CHICKA-ROCKA-BOOM, Jen.

Jen? I say BOOM-CHICKA-ROCKA-BOOM, Jen?

Jen   –

Birdie   BOOM-CHICKA-ROCKA-BOOM, Adira?

Adira? BOOM-CHICKA-ROCKA-BOOM?

Adira   –

Birdie   Lots of energy, guys, yeah come on? Lots of upbeat positive energy.

Adira   –

Birdie   OK, Orson, I'm not gonna even bother.

Franny.

BOOM-CHICKA-ROCKA-BOOM, Franny.

Yeah? Like that do you, Franny? Want some of Birdie's energy?

Franny   –

Birdie   Ooo, careful, who knows where I might go
next, Tana?

It could be anyone, Tana.

Where am I gonna go next, Tana?

BOOM-CHICKA-ROCKA-BOOM, Tana. Yes!

Tana   –

Birdie   No?

Lots of energy, come on let's get you all up on your feet and
energised, Jotham, you love this one, I know you do. Don't
leave me hanging, Jotham, I'm looking to you. Ready? Let's
do it, come on Jotham. Energy, eye contact, cool, yeah?

Jotham, ready, this one's for you.

I say BOOM-CHICKA-ROCKA-BOOM.

Orson   Don't do it, Jotham.

Birdie   BOOM-CHICKA-ROCKA-BOOM.

Orson   Stay strong.

Birdie   I say BOOM-CHICKA-ROCKA-BOOM, Jotham.

Orson   Don't let her break you.

Birdie   BOOM-CHICKA-ROCKA-BOOM, Jotham.

BOOM-CHICKA-ROCKA-BOOM, Jotham.

Orson   This is what she does. She picks off a weak one.

Birdie   BOOM-CHICKA-ROCKA-BOOM, Jotham.

Orson   Jotham.

Birdie   BOOM-CHICKA-ROCKA-BOOM.

Orson   Jotham.

Birdie   BOOM-CHICKA-ROCKA-BOOM.

Orson   No, Jotham.

Birdie   I say BOOM-CHICKA-ROCKA-BOOM, Jotham.

Orson   Don't let her beat you.

Birdie   BOOM-CHICKA-ROCKA-BOOM.

BOOM-CHICKA-ROCKA-BOOM.

You want to.

Don't you? Don't you, Jotham?

Yeah?

You want it?

It's coming.

Birdie's coming.

BOOM-CHICKA-ROCKA-BOOM, Jotham.

That's what I say, Jotham.

Orson   Stay strong, Jotham,

Birdie   I say BOOM-CHICKA-ROCKA-BOOM.

Orson   This is bigger than you.

Birdie   BOOM-CHIKCA-ROCKA-BOOM, Jotham.

Orson   Eyes on me, Jotham.

Birdie   BOOM-CHICKA-ROCKA-BOOM, JOTHAM!

Orson   Look at me.

Birdie   BOOM-CHICKA-ROCKA-BOOM, JOTHAM!

Orson   Resist.

Birdie   BOOM-CHICKA-ROCKA-BOOM HE WANTS IT.

Orson   Stay strong. Eyes on me.

Birdie   BOOM-CHICKA-ROCKA-BOOM, JOTHAM!

Orson   No!

Birdie   BOOM-CHICKA-ROCKA-BOOM.

Orson   Jotham, no!

Jotham   I say boom-chicka-rocka-boom.

Birdie   YES! YES YOU DO.

YES YOU DO BLOODY SAY IT. THAT'S WHAT I'M
TALKING ABOUT. COME ON!

Orson   You're weak.

Birdie   BOOM-CHICKA-ROCKA-BOOM, Jotham.

Jotham   I say BOOM-CHICKA-ROCKA-BOOM, Birdie.

Birdie   Now we're rolling.

BOOM-CHICKA-ROCKA-BOOM, Jen.

Jen   You won't break me.

Birdie   Oh yeah?

Orson   Dig deep, Jen.

Birdie   Boom-chicka-shut-your-face, Orson.

Adira   Please, make it stop.

Birdie   This is your meeting, guys.

Your space; your meeting.

This feels good doesn't it? All of us connecting and
communicating, alert, full of energy.

Woo! Yeah!

OK, so what I'm hearing you say is that /

Adira   That this is shit.

Birdie   I'm hearing you say you all really enjoyed the
icebreaker.

She finds her agenda.

Fun and hilarious icebreaker.

Tick.

Everyone energised and ready to participate.

Tick.

Item two.

Emus.

I can't read my writing.

Oh yes: emotions.

Does anyone have any emotions?

Adira   I'd like to kill myself.

Birdie   Right that's quite a biggie there, Adira, not sure we're all ready or qualified for that. Any alternative emotion you're feeling other than the one you just said that you could share instead?

Adira   Nope, it's mainly just that one.

Birdie   Well, maybe just park that for now, OK, Adira?

Lovely.

What about you, Jen?

Jen   –

Birdie   Jotham?

Jotham   –

Birdie   Adira?

Adira   –

Birdie   Any emotions, Franny? Any at all?

Franny   –

Birdie   Any emotions from anyone at all?

Do we need a reminder of the ground rules?

Number four: 'Make a positive contribution.'

I'm here to facilitate you making a positive a contribution.

Adira, you sure?

Adira   –

Birdie   Fine.

OK, let's do another icebreaker.

Groans.

Tana   Can someone please shoot me?

Adira   Count yourself lucky you don't actually live here.

Birdie   OK, then, fine, let's just sit in silence and you won't be heard and you won't get a say in how we do things at Spectrum, and sod you all, sod the lot of you,

I mean it.

Thank you.

So let's get back to the agenda.

I have convened this meeting because of last night's incident.

Orson   Where's Sally?

Birdie   Sally is on annual leave.

Orson   So we can't have a meeting then.

Birdie   Yes we can.

Orson   You're not allowed to take meetings unsupervised.

Birdie   Not true.

Orson   Are you qualified yet?

Birdie   No.

Orson   There you go.

Birdie Sally said it's fine.

Sally said I'm more than capable of taking this meeting on my own. And given there's a deadline, we have to have it now.

Orson Yes, but /

Birdie More than capable, Orson.

Sally's words not mine.

And I'm the oldest.

Orson Only by two months.

Birdie I'm not a teenager anymore and all you lot still are and a lot can happen in two months that makes someone more mature.

Jen Like getting fingered by Becky Both-Ways behind Lidl?

Birdie I don't discuss my private life with residents, it's unprofessional.

Orson But you'll lock yourself in the bathroom and cry when Becky Both-Ways goes back to her boyfriend.

Very professional.

Birdie It was painful.

Jotham Her fingers aren't that big.

Birdie Emotionally painful.

Jotham ET phone home.

Birdie Let's all have a good laugh at my suffering, thanks, great right let's move on.

We need to agree the agenda.

TV rota, washing-up rota, we'll do at the end. We have bigger fingers – fish, we have bigger fish to fry.

After last night's debacle, I want us to get this thing sorted once and for all.

Jotham   We all go as Disney princesses.

Orson   This is a silent protest.

Tana   How come you're talking then?

Birdie   I don't mean the theme for Bournemouth Pride, Jotham. We'll have to park that till next meeting.

You're all going to have to talk to each other again at some point.

Orson   They're not talking because they're protesting against you, Birdie.

Birdie   They're not talking because they all blame each other for there being no wifi.

And if we ever have a scene like last night again, I'll switch it off for a month.

So let's get to business.

As you've all seen fit to discuss it on social media, but can't seem to discuss it face to face, we're going to all put our phones in this box and you don't get them back till we have agreed how you will commemorate the two minutes' silence.

It's happening like literally in half an hour, and we need to agree what we're doing.

Orson   We don't have time.

Jen   I've got a test to revise for.

Birdie   All phones in the box please.

Jotham   What if we miss it?

Birdie   Set your alarm for thirty minutes' time, Jotham.

Adira   I'm not sitting here with these idiots for half an hour. I'm not talking to them anyway.

Jen   No one's talking to you either.

Jotham   I am.

Tana   Me too.

Jotham   I'm only not talking to Orson cos he slagged off Bournemouth Pride and Bournemouth Pride is amazing.

Franny, who are you not talking to?

Franny   –

Jotham   Right.

Adira   I'm not talking to anyone but I'm talking to Jotham a little bit.

Jen   If she's not talking to me, I'm not talking to her.

And how come she's allowed to eat her dinner in her room and we're not?

Birdie   Adira, you're our newest arrival, so I don't expect you to know, but here at Spectrum, we sort things out by talking.

Orson   As our longest member I can tell you we sort absolutely nothing out by talking cos Birdie's in charge.

Birdie   We do sort things by talking actually.

Jotham   Yeah and not by emptying the kitchen bin in my bed.

Adira   That wasn't me.

Jen   Who was it then?

Birdie   I'm going to interview you all separately about it and for the record, Orson, how do you think we got the washing-up rota if it wasn't by talking, or the TV rota, or the food-labelling system?

Jen   We hate all those things.

Orson   Yes, hence our silent protest.

Birdie   But for now, we've got one agenda item and one agenda item only.

It's happening up and down the county, all over the world in fact. You want to be left out?

I know it happened a long way away. But we need to agree on how we're going to commemorate it.

So, phones please.

Groans.

Come on. They're not actually attached to you.

See, look. They detach from our bodies and everything. Oh my God it's not actually a claw, it's a hand.

Come on.

You know the rules.

She walks round with the box. With great difficulty, each parts with his/her/their phone.

Alarm set, Jotham?

Jotham Yep.

Tana That's my phone.

Jotham Mum gave it to me when she confiscated it from you.

Tana I'm taking it back with me.

Jen It's his phone now.

Tana Stop listening to our conversation.

Jen You're in a communal space actually.

Tana Yeah? Well it's a private conversation.

Adira No such thing in this place.

Jotham You lost it when you lied to Mum about going to that party so it's mine now.

Alarm is set.

And can we hurry up so we can talk about the Pride costumes?

Birdie Not today, Jotham.

Jotham It's not you who's got to make them.

Birdie Jotham, I mean it. This is more important.

Jotham OK, fine.

Go.

He sets his alarm and the phone goes off.

Birdie Great, let's get this sorted once and for all.

Orson Can't you lot remember anything? We're supposed to be doing a silent protest.

Birdie No one gives a toss what you think, Orson.

Orson I don't give you permission to speak to me like that.

Birdie Like what?

Orson I call that a very rude remark indeed.

Birdie Oh do you?

Orson It's not appropriate for the youth empowerment mentors to speak to residents like that.

Sally wouldn't like it.

Birdie Sally's not here, are they?

Orson Do we need a reminder of the ground rules, Birdie?

Birdie Oh piss off.

Orson Number one: 'Everyone is entitled to be treated with respect.'

And can I just say, I felt very disempowered when you told me to piss off just now.

I felt shamed.

Birdie   Orson, can I speak to you in my office please?

Orson   You don't have an office.

Birdie   Can you step into my office please?

Orson   It's not an office.

Birdie   Yes it is.

Orson   No it's not.

Birdie   Yes it is.

Orson   It's a broom cupboard.

Birdie   It's a multi-purpose room, can you come please?

Orson   Into that room with the mop and bucket?

Birdie   And a chair and a desk and a computer and wifi.

Jotham   When can we have the wifi code again?

Birdie   When Caia's done the washing-up. And when you lot start talking to each other again.

Jen   How can she wash up when she's working all the time?

Jotham   Where is she?

Jen   Working, numbnuts.

Orson   This room here with the dustpan and brush?

Birdie   What do you want?

Orson   And bin bags and bleach and the poster of /

Birdie   What do you want?

Orson   Aha. So you acknowledge our protest.

Birdie   What protest?

Orson   This one.

Birdie   Against me?

Orson   We demand change.

Birdie   Of what?

Orson   This oppressive regime.

Birdie   Me?

But I'm nice.

I'm Birdie.

Orson   I have an announcement.

In the spirit of those who came before me: Emmeline Pankhurst. Harvey Milk. Marsha P. Johnson.

And some others.

I stand here before you and say, 'We protest'.

Enough is enough.

Birdie   Enough of what?

Orson   This is a takedown.

I'm going to dismantle you, Birdie.

Slowly, painfully, publicly.

I'm going to take you down.

Birdie   Is that a fact now?

Orson   Yes.

Birdie   You think you've got what it takes?

Orson   Oh yes.

And more.

Birdie   Got what it takes to come for me do you, Orson?

Orson   I've got what it takes to come for you, Birdie

Birdie   OK, let's go.

Orson   Let's go where?

Birdie   Let's go, figuratively, let's go as in you think you've got what it takes, so let's go.

Orson   Where do you wanna go, Birdie? Into the broom cupboard.

Birdie   Take the piss out of my multi-purpose room again, go on, do it and let's see what happens.

Tana   OK, stop.

Orson   This is a silent protest, Tana.

Birdie   Well shut your mouth then, Orson.

Tana   It's bullying.

Birdie   I'm not bullying him.

Tana   He's bullying you.

Birdie   I'm not being bullied.

Tana   Yes you are.

Birdie   No I'm not.

Tana   You are.

Orson   Tana, it's a silent protest.

Tana   Let's vote.

Hands up if you think Orson is bullying Birdie.

Orson   You don't even live here.

Tana   Hands up.

Birdie   This isn't on the agenda.

Tana   Who thinks Orson is bullying Birdie?

Everyone puts up his/her/their hands.

Birdie   He's not.

He's really not. I'm fine, guys, honestly.

What Orson is doing is a good example of 'acting out'.

Orson   Learn that in college this week did you?

Birdie   Orson is not happy with himself as a person, there are bits about himself he doesn't like and instead of saying, let me take ownership of that, he's come in and acted out.

And maybe I did learn it and you can't handle it because I'm the year above you and you don't know about it yet and you don't like that do you?

You can't handle me, can you?

You can't handle Birdie.

Orson   This is a coup, the ground rules no longer apply.

Birdie   The ground rules always apply.

And you guys wrote them yourselves, including you, Orson: your signature's on the bottom too. So sit down please and let's carry on.

Orson   REVOLUTION.

Birdie   Yes, Orson.

Orson   RAGE. REVOLUTION. REVOLT.

Shout it with me, everyone. RAGE, REVOLUTION, REVOLT.

Adira   Orson, you pressured us into not speaking and I'm not cool with that so sit down and shut up and let's get this dumb meeting over.

Orson   The ground rules, remember.

RAGE /

Adira   Do you want to eat the ground /

Orson   REVOLUTION /

Adira   – rules, Orson, cos I'll rip them off the wall and /

Orson   REVOLT.

Birdie   Right, stop!

We get it, Orson.

Thank you.

OK.

Right, can we carry on now please?

Back to the agenda.

Enter **Caia** *dressed as Ronald McDonald.*

Caia   Who took my burgers away?

Where is the Hamburglar? I'm going to find them.

Orson   Who the hell are you?

Caia   I'm Ronald McDonald.

Who the hell are you?

Orson   We're in the middle of a coup here.

Caia   A coup!

How thrilling.

My, don't we all look sad.

Birdie   Can we have just one house meeting without all this, please?

Caia   You, girl.

Jen   Me?

Caia   Yes, you.

Caia   Why are you so sad?

Jen   Why is Ronald McDonald talking to me?

Caia   Ronald McDonald will not be silenced!

He comes with a message.

On this day, a day when love wins over hate, a day of coming together, a day of unity, a day of communities rising up all over the globe, in one bright voice, Ronald McDonald brings a message of hope.

Birdie   Yes, babes.

Orson   RAGE. REVOLUTION.

Adira   Orson, do you have to do this every day?

Birdie   Orson can choose *not* to do this every day if he likes.

Caia   A message of hope, guys.

Birdie   And if you are planning a coup, you need to put that in writing with twenty-four hours' advance warning and we need to do a risk assessment.

Caia   Ronald McDonald will not be silenced!

You will hear him.

But you shall not fear him.

Birdie   OK, can we all listen to Ronald McDonald's message of hope please?

Just a *quick* message of hope though please, Mr McDonald.

Jotham   When are you lot gonna fix that window?

Birdie   Thank you, Jotham, for using this space appropriately.

I'm happy you felt empowered and able to voice your concern safely.

Jotham   Just answer the question.

Orson   Yes, can you answer that please? Or is it more evidence of how you're unfit to lead this group?

Adira   They'll only smash it again.

Birdie   So we'll repair it.

Jotham   Yeah, then they'll smash it again.

Birdie   Let them.

It's not gonna ruin *my* day.

We'll repair it.

Jen   We should spend the money on something else.

Birdie   They're coming this afternoon.

Tana   Just board it up, then they can't smash it anymore.

Birdie   We're not doing that.

Tana   Why?

Birdie   If we leave it, it says this is OK, this is how we accept being treated.

We fix it because we fix it. No matter how many times they smash it.

Jen   It's a waste of money.

Birdie   There are other things we could spend it on, I agree.

Adira   Like better food.

Birdie   Like better food, or a trip to Bournemouth Pride, whatever.

Caia   Or a dishwasher.

Jen   They'll just keep on smashing it.

Tana   Why don't you put a CCTV camera up?

Birdie   We can't afford it.

Jen   Cos we spent the budget on fixing the window.

Caia   Silence, I say!

Ronald McDonald is experiencing an emotion.

Birdie   An emotion? Brilliant!

Don't panic, I'm coming.

Birdie's here, she's ready.

Tell Birdie, she's got you.

Caia   There is sadness in Ronald McDonald's heart.

Biride   Sadness. Amazing! That's great, really brilliant.

Everyone hear that? Ronald McDonald is sad, isn't that wonderful?

Anyone else?

Caia   Ronald McDonald is sad because a dear friend of his has been spurned.

Ruthlessly, callously, spurned.

Birdie   Great, Ronald, really great, tell Birdie all about it.

Caia   Isn't that right, Franny?

Jotham   What about the window?

Birdie   It will be fixed today, let's move on.

Caia   Hasn't she, Franny?

Adira   Franny, did you spurn Ronald?

Caia   No, not Ronald! No one spurns Ronald McDonald.

She has spurned one of Ronald's friends. And now she won't even speak to her.

To punish her.

Jotham   Caia, we know it's you.

Jen   She knows we know.

Birdie   Caia, can you pack it in now please?

We need to decide what we'll do for the silence.

Caia   Silence!

Birdie   No obviously silence, the question was /

Caia   No I mean: SILENCE!

Ronald must be heard.

Franny won't even speak to Ronald's friend who she callously spurned.

So, if Franny isn't talking to Caia.

Perhaps she will talk to Caia's dear and trusted friend Ronald McDonald and tell him what Caia did wrong?

Even just the tiniest clue would be helpful.

Tell Ronald McDonald all about it.

Why won't you speak to Caia?

Orson   Can I ask the group leader what her plan is to get this meeting back on track cos she seems out of her depth.

Birdie   Caia stroke Ronald McDonald and Franny. Stay behind at the end and I will facilitate a conversation between the pair of you.

Caia   I need to know now.

Franny, what did I do?

I'm dying.

Jen   Is this all you could think of?

Caia   Franny.

Beautiful, rare, gleaming pebble that you are.

I would never have said it if I thought it would upset you.

Jen   What did you say?

Birdie   This is a private conversation, you two. Maybe you should wait till you have privacy?

We need to make a decision about the silence.

Does anyone have any thoughts?

Orson   Yes.

Birdie   Anyone have any thoughts?

Orson   I do.

Birdie   Anyone at all.

Orson   Yeah, me.

Birdie   Anyone at all.

Orson   I have thoughts.

Birdie   Absolutely anyone at all.

Orson   My thought is we all go outside.

Birdie   Adira, what do you think?

Orson   She thinks we all go out together.

Adira   No I don't.

Orson   All out together.

Jen   No.

Orson   Yes.

Jen   No.

Caia   This how it's been, Birdie.

Orson   We all go out together.

Caia   Not everyone wants to do that, Orson.

Orson   Yes they do.

Adira   No we don't.

Birdie   Caia, what do you want to do?

Caia   I want to go out, hold my Franny's hand and show the world I love her and that I'm not scared and that being in love is awesome and my love is as good as theirs and I want to kiss her in the sun with the whole world watching.

That's what I want to do.

Jotham   It's raining.

Birdie   Franny?

Caia   She's not talking.

Birdie   To you? Or to all of us?

Caia   It started off me but I think she's extended the protest to society as a whole.

Birdie   What are you protesting about, Franny?

Franny   –

Caia   She's protesting that I asked her to marry me.

Tana   Oh my God that's so cute.

Caia   I know, right? I got down on one knee and everything.

Jen   Oh my God, that's so lame.

Caia   And I know the ring was a bit naff but the man in H. Samuel's said it was the best I was gonna get at my price point and one day I'll buy a nicer one, but also, who cares? Who cares about a ring?

Jotham   I do.

Adira   You've got to have a ring.

Jotham   I know, right?

When my man proposes to me, I want a flash mob.

Adira   Why should he propose to you?

Jotham   Cos he's the man.

Adira   But you're a man too.

Jotham   Yeah, but I'm the fabulous one.

Caia   Who cares about all that? I'm trying to tell you what happened.

Jen   No one cares.

Tana   I do.

Tell the story, Caia.

Caia   It's not a story. It's a tragedy.

Jotham   Stories can be tragedies.

Jen   Your hair's a tragedy.

Jotham   Your life's a tragedy.

Caia   Listen to me.

Jotham   The alarm's gonna go off.

Caia   If you all stopped interrupting me –

Adira   Can't you say it in 140 characters?

Caia   And we got the train to Dungeness and I got down on one knee on England's only desert that looks dead but it's secretly teeming with /

Adira   That's a no then.

Caia   Teeming with life and I said, 'Franny, I can't live without you'.

Adira   What is she? Your phone charger?

Caia   And we stood in the shadow of the power station and it was windy and I said, 'Franny, isn't love wonderful? Isn't it badass and brilliant and we've got it, so many people don't have it, we have love Franny, and Franny, will you marry me?' That's all I said.

Jen   No wonder she said no.

Caia   She didn't say no.

Tana   Did she say yes?

Caia   She didn't say anything.

She's not spoken since.

I'm dying cos I'm in Hell: it's like Primark on a Saturday;
then Franny texted, didn't you my shiny pebble, she texted
to say she feels marriage is – hold on, I've still got the text,
and yeah that's right . . . marriage is an oppressive
institution.

Tana   What does that mean?

Caia   Exactly, Tana.

What does it mean?

Jen   How come her phone doesn't have to go in the box?

Caia   But she says I should have known that because if I'd
known that –

Oh God oh God oh God oh I lay myself at your feet, Franny.

FRANNY.

I will drown in the sea. I will do it. I will walk into the sea
and not come back.

Birdie   OK, so why don't we just park that?

Adira   Come sit here, Caia.

Caia   Thank you, Adira.

Kind, compassionate Adira.

Adira   It's fine.

Caia   I'll just sit here and weep.

Or maybe I'll just die.

Is that what you want, Franny? Do you want me to die from
the pain of loving you?

Franny   –

Caia   She doesn't deny it.

Jotham   I think she just wants you to stop talking shit.

Birdie   OK. So we're good?

Can we carry on?

Tana   What about the coup?

Jotham   TANA!

Birdie   He'd forgotten about it.

Jen   Oh no.

Orson   NEVER FORGET!

Jotham   Go hang out with your imaginary boyfriend, Orson.

Orson   RAGE, he's not imaginary actually, Jotham, REVOLUTION, just cos you haven't seen him doesn't mean he doesn't exist, REVOLT.

Jen   He's Mister 'Out and Proud', but won't show us his boyfriend.

Orson   RAAAAAAGE!

Birdie   THAT IS ENOUGH!

You want rage?

You wanna see a little bit of Birdie's rage?

I got rage. I got rage in spades and you don't want to know what your life will be like with Birdie's rage all up in your face.

So let's park the coup.

Let's park the Ross and Rachel.

Caia *puts up her hand.*

Birdie   And can we actually discuss what we're here to discuss, because time is running out and /

What, Caia? What?

Caia   I think it was very insensitive to choose such a hetero-normative example.

Birdie   Of what?

Caia   I'm not comfortable with being compared to a cis-hetero couple.

Jen   Who the hell are Ross and Rachel?

Tana   They were these dickheads in the olden days.

Caia   Proper dickheads.

Birdie   You're right. I am sorry.

Caia and Franny and anyone else, anyone else at all, including Ronald McDonald, I apologise for my insensitive choice of language. I have listened to your comments and taken the time to reflect on my own privilege and I am sorry if anyone felt devalued or shamed by my lapse of judgement.

OK?

Good.

We need to make a decision and what I am hearing is that you want to go outside.

Orson   Finally some leadership.

Jen   I'm not going out.

Jotham   Nor am I.

Adira   Nope.

Orson   What is wrong with you?

Jen   Nothing's wrong with me.

What's wrong with *you*?

Orson   We have to get out there.

Adira   I don't.

Orson   You're letting them win.

Birdie   It's not as simple as that.

Caia   It is. It so is.

Tana Why do you all have to do the same thing?

Adira I know, right?

Birdie Solidarity.

Orson Solidarity.

You're still an unfit leader though.

Birdie We're spectrum.

We commemorate as a group.

Jen We don't want to.

Birdie But it matters that we do.

Jotham No it doesn't.

Orson I'm sorry, but it does. It absolutely does matter.

People out there want to divide us. And turn us against each other so they can have power over us. That's how they win.

But solidarity is a bond that unites us. It says I'm not scared because I've got you, and you're not scared because you've got me.

It matters because there are people very far away from us who are living in fear, more than we ever have or will, and we need to say to them, you don't need to be scared because you've got us.

We've got them and they've got us.

Jotham Outside: no. But as a group, yes.

Tana When is it?

Birdie In exactly twenty-one minutes' time.

Tana Jotham, my train leaves at quarter past.

Jotham So?

Tana You said you'd walk me to the station.

Jotham   Well, I can't now.

Tana   You promised.

Jotham   I want to do the silence.

Tana   I hardly see you.

Jotham   Then get a later train.

Tana   Mum bought the tickets and I have to get the train it says on my ticket.

Jotham   I'm only worth the cheapest. Thanks, Mum.

Tana   Why should we have to pay the earth just to see you?

Birdie   Tana, I think this is a private conversation.

Tana   Nothing's private in this place. I've only been here a night and I know way more about you lot than I want to.

Pack your bags and come home to Mum and Dad.

Birdie   Do you think you might be being a bit insensitive in saying that to your brother, Tana?

Tana   Stop putting ideas in his head.

Birdie   I'm not.

Tana   You're turning him against his family.

Jotham   No she's not.

Tana   You shouldn't be here, with people like him coming out with crap like that.

All that rubbish about solidarity?

What about solidarity with your family?

Jotham   This is my family.

Tana   This lot?

This lot?

Caia   What's wrong with us?

Tana You're in the bloody funny farm.

Caia Speak for yourself, I'm fine.

Tana I just meant /

Jotham I'm not going home.

Orson Why don't you get a later train? They don't check your tickets down here.

Tana I don't want to get another train. I want to do what my brother and I agreed and not to have bloody group therapy about it.

Jotham?

Jotham Are we doing it inside or outside cos if /

Caia Out and proud.

Adira No.

Birdie Can we at least agree we'll do it as a group?

Orson We have to do it as a group.

Caia Franny?

Franny –

Caia Cool.

Birdie Jen?

Jen What?

Birdie We'll do it as a group, yeah?

Jen –

Birdie Jen.

Jen –

Birdie Jen, you /

Jen I don't think she should be allowed to pray.

Birdie   Who?

Jen   Her.

Birdie   Jen, that's /

Jen   Adira, are you going to pray during the two minutes' silence?

Birdie   Jen, it's not OK to ask that.

Jen   I'm not being disrespectful, Adira, are you gonna pray?

Jotham   So what if she does?

Tana   Jotham, let's go.

Jen   I don't want to be in some prayer circle. If she prays I want to be separate.

Caia   Who cares what she does?

Jen   It's insensitive.

Birdie   You're the one being insensitive.

Jen   I'm not being rude, but I'm not doing it.

You lot, do what you want, but I'm not doing a prayer circle.

Tana   Are you gonna pray, Adira?

Birdie   Don't answer, babes.

Adira   Why can't I answer?

Orson   She means you don't have to answer, but she's an incompetent group leader.

Birdie   Right. No. Sorry.

Adira, we'll come back to you in a minute, but there's a really good learning opportunity here and it's important I role model appropriate levels of self-esteem, so Orson, would you come into my office please?

Orson   What office?

Birdie   Over there in the /

Orson   All I can see is a broom cupboard.

Birdie   You're just angry cos you don't have an office.

Orson   *You* don't have an office.

Birdie   It's a multi-purpose room. And come on, let's say it, we all know what this is about.

Orson   You wanna do this here.

Birdie   Let's go, Face-ache.

Orson   No one here needs you, Birdie.

Birdie   Yes they do.

Orson   You're not helping anyone.

Jotham   She's helped me.

Orson   No she's not. She's making you worse.

Jotham   Birdie was really nice to me.

Orson   If you say you want to stay inside, Birdie has failed you.

Birdie   No.

Orson   We should be taking to the streets, fight them head on, full out, but you're like, no, let's all stay in and hide.

Caia   I'm not hiding.

Orson   You're dressed as Ronald McDonald!

And look at these windows, how can you say you're not hiding?

Caia   I'm not hiding.

Orson   You're all hiding.

Tana   I'm not.

Orson   What have you got to hide from?

Tana   I'm booked on a train so let's /

Orson   What is more important? Supporting your brother or getting home on time?

Things are changing. Everything is changing, but you can't see it because you can't see out past these damn windows.

Birdie   We know things are changing. We did a wall display about it.

She points to a wall display entitled 'Things are Changing'.

Orson   'Don't be too out there.'

Birdie   Who said that?

Orson   You do. Every day.

Birdie   No I don't, and even if I did, don't you think that's sensible?

Orson   Locking yourselves away.

Birdie   When I lived here we couldn't even open the curtains.

Orson   You think this is progress?

A bit of sunlight.

Birdie   It *is* progress.

Orson   It's not.

It's not, Birdie.

You're going backwards.

Birdie   I know you resent being here.

Orson   I hate it here.

Adira   Me too.

Tana   And me.

Jotham   You don't have to live here.

Tana   Nor do you.

Adira   How can you expect him to go home?

Tana   Who, him?

Adira   How can he go home?

Tana   You just get on a train, it's not hard.

Birdie   Everyone hates it here, great.

Caia   I don't.

Birdie   You love everything, Caia.

Orson   Why do you give a crap if everyone likes you or not?

Birdie   I don't.

Orson   You need everyone to like you.

Well, newsflash, we think you're an armpit.

Birdie   You don't like it here, OK, fine, you've made that clear but don't make it personal please.

Orson   She's done one term of a youth work diploma and this is how she goes on.

Birdie   And what have you done?

Orson   You're not qualified to do this.

Birdie   Sorry, Orson, what youth work qualifications do you have?

Orson   None.

Birdie   Exactly.

And furthermore, I used to be a resident here. I painted these walls.

Orson   'Been there, done that' is not a qualification.

How do you think it makes them feel when you say you've all got to hide away?

Birdie   I'm not saying that.

Orson   You are.

Birdie   I'm not. I'm saying you've got a choice.

Orson   As long as everyone does it together.

Birdie   I would like it for us all to do it together, yes.

Orson   Inside.

Birdie   Wherever we want, I don't mind.

Orson   You should mind. If you were doing your job you'd say we've got to get out and be seen, show them we're not ashamed.

All these laws they made against us, they told us we were disgusting. We've got to say, we're not, we know we're not.

The love I feel for my boyfriend is not disgusting.

Get out, be seen, Birdie.

Get up in their faces, not run back into the closet.

Birdie   *It's a multi-purpose room.*

Orson   The 'closet' closet. This lot are the sheep and you're the dog rounding them all up.

Birdie   You can't even be seen out with your boyfriend.

Orson   I just don't bring him here, that's different.

Adira   Because he's not real.

Jotham   I don't want to go outside.

Birdie   You don't have to.

Orson   Yes you do.

Jotham, yes you do. Because if you don't, they've won.

You too, Adira, and you, Jen.

Where's the fight? Where's the pride? Where's the shoulders back, chest out, come for me pride?

Jen   I left mine at home.

Adira   My dog ate it.

Orson   This isn't funny.

I get that you're scared. But this is bigger than you.

And what is that fear?

What actually is it?

You're scared because of what they'll say? They've already said it.

You're scared of what they might do? They've already done it.

So that fear, it's based on what *might* happen, but everything that might happen already has.

So what does that tell you?

Jotham   It tells me I'm never gonna get a boyfriend.

Orson   It tells you there's nothing left to be afraid of.

Jotham   Oh, and that.

Orson   There's nothing left to be afraid of, guys.

Adira   That's so easy for you to say, Orson.

Not all of us have your life.

Jen   No one cares, Adira.

Birdie   I do.

Jen   Maybe you should say a prayer, see where that gets you.

Jotham   OK, you need to stop.

Jen   Are you going to pray, Adira?

Jotham   Leave her alone, Jen.

Adira   I can handle her.

Jotham   When are you two gonna get a room and be done with it?

Jen   I don't wanna get a room with her.

Adira   Gross.

Jotham   Adira, Jen is so into you, it's off the scale.

Jen   Are you gonna pray?

Jotham   That's it, change the subject.

Adira   Of course I'm gonna pray.

Jen   This is what I mean.

They don't give a shit about us.

Adira   I get it, Jen.

The attacker looked like me and attacked people like you.

Jen   Well, didn't they?

Adira   I'm not disagreeing.

Jen   What's your point then?

Adira   What's my point? On behalf of who? People like me? People like you? People like us?

Who gives a toss what my point is?

It's way worse for people like me after these things, I can tell you.

Jen   People like you did it.

Jotham   Shut up, Jen.

Jen   No.

Jotham   You're talking shit, Jen.

Caia   Seriously, Jen.

Aren't you gonna kick her out, Birdie?

Jen   *She* should get out.

Adira, can you leave please?

This is my safe space and you're making me feel uncomfortable.

Jotham   Shut your mouth, Jen.

Caia   Jen, you're being awful.

Jen   Get out, Adira.

You're the one that should leave.

Orson   Hey, Birdie, great job. I can't wait to tell Sally how you handled this.

Birdie   That's enough.

The ground rules clearly state that /

Orson   It's a bit late for that, don't you think, Birdie?

Jen   Every member of Spectrum has a right to be here without fear of persecution – number two /

Birdie   Every member has a right to be themselves – number eight.

Jen   Every member has a right to speak freely – number six.

Orson   We can all read.

Birdie's not got the balls, so I'll do it.

Jen, get out.

Jen   I'm not going anywhere.

Birdie   Hold on guys, we can't just /

Jen   This is my safe space. You're gonna kick me out? You know how vulnerable I am.

Birdie   You lose that right when you make comments like that.

Orson   Better late than never, Birdie.

Birdie   Leave now please, I'll make an appointment with you and we can talk about next steps.

Orson   Oh, I wouldn't do it like that.

Birdie   Right, you can leave too Orson.

Adira   I told you I can handle it.

Honestly, you lot do my head in.

Let Jen stay.

I'm done with the lot of you anyway.

Tana   Jotham, come on.

Adira   What time is your train, Tana?

Tana   Quarter past.

Adira   Mind if I come with you?

Jen   Are you leaving?

Adira   Why would I want to stay here with people like you?

Jen   You can't just leave.

Birdie   Jen didn't mean what she said.

Tana   Will you be safe?

Adira   I don't care about what Jen said.

I'm sorry, but I literally can't stay here any longer.

I'll just grab a bag and send my brothers down for my stuff.

Can I come with you, Tana?

Jotham   Are we allowed to just leave?

Caia   This isn't prison, Jotham.

Adira   Yes it bloody is.

Birdie   We need to talk to your social worker, Adira.

Caia   But Adira, we love you.

Birdie   We do.

Jotham   Jen really does.

Adira   I don't want your love. No offence.

I want Mum's love. And Dad's love and my brothers'.

Birdie   They need time, babes.

Adria   They've had time.

More than enough time.

Jen   What if they kick you out again?

Adira   I'm not coming back here if they do.

Birdie   You need to think this through.

Adira   I have.

Birdie   You can leave, but why don't we plan it?

Go home for a weekend at a time; build up it slowly.

Adira   I'd rather just do it and be done.

Birdie   I don't think that's a good idea.

Caia   Will you add me on Facebook?

Adira   I'll add you all.

Birdie   Adira, I can't stop you.

But you don't need to rush off.

Adira   Yeah I do.

I'm sorry but I'm done.

I'm so done.

And you can't stop me.

Birdie   I'm not stopping you.

Adira   You are.

Birdie   Plan it. Don't rush. That's what I'm saying.

Adira   I don't want to.

I want to go home now.

Don't pressure me to do something I don't want to do.

Birdie   OK.

If it's your choice, I stand by you.

But I want you to know that we really do wish you well.

And whatever happens, you know we'll always be here.

Adira   Thanks yeah.

But do you have any idea how depressing that is?

This place is shit and, no offence, you're all twats.

I miss my mum. And she's not here, she's there.

And I know what she said.

She said she wished I was dead, that having a gay child was worse than death. I know she said that.

But even so –

Jotham, you know what I mean.

Tana   Why would Jotham understand that?

Adira   And Orson, you say revolution but /

Tana   No hold on.

Jotham?

Why would you get that?

Caia   There's not enough love, that's what I think.

Tana   What's my brother said to you?

Adira, what's he told you?

Adira   –

Tana   What's he told you?

Jotham   Forget it.

Tana   No.

Jotham   Leave it.

Tana   What have you said?

Jotham   I've not said nothing.

Tana   Then why did she say /

Adira   I didn't say /

Tana   Yeah you did.

Jotham   I said leave it, OK?

Tana   No.

Birdie   Tana, your brother clearly /

Tana   Stay out of my family's business.

Birdie   We have a confidentiality agreement.

Tana   You're talking about my family.

Adira   I wasn't.

Tana   You said, 'Jotham, you get it'.

Jotham   Tana, please.

Tana   I have a right to know what's been said about me.

Caia   No one said anything.

Tana   Bullshit, what has he said about us?

Jotham   I haven't said nothing.

Tana   Yeah you have.

Jotham   You're humiliating me.

Tana   What about me?

Jotham   You're gonna miss your train, let's go.

Tana   No don't worry, we're talking, it's nice.

Jotham   Please.

Tana   What has my brother said?

Can someone please answer my question?

Answer me.

Silence.

Eventually –

Adira   He said /

Birdie   Ground rules, Adira.

Adira   He said your mum and dad kicked him out.

When he came out your dad beat the crap out of him.

Which is what happened to me. So we kind of bonded over it.

Tana   He said that?

Is that what he said?

Birdie   Adira, that /

Adira   It's family, Birdie.

Tana   Jotham, get your stuff and we'll go.

If we get a taxi we'll just make it.

Jotham   –

He may be crying.

Tana   Jotham, come on.

You lot are twats.

My brother's coming with me.

Adira   Can I share your cab?

Tana   Anyone else want to get out of this dump?

Jotham   It's not a dump, Tana.

It's my home.

Tana   *It's not your home, Jotham.*

These freaks are not your family.

Orson   Hey.

Tana   You're freaks. You're mental and you're turning him away from his family.

Birdie   You need to leave now please, Tana.

Orson   Are we all leaving? There'll be no one left.

Good job, Birdie.

Jen   We're not turning him away from his mum and dad, Tana. They turned away from him.

Tana   How the hell would you know?

Jotham   Please don't.

Tana   We went to *Wicked*.

Pizza Express, then *Wicked*.

Do you know what that took for my mum and dad to do that?

Have you seen *Wicked*?

It's shit.

It's got singing monkeys, what's all that about?

But do you know what it took for my mum and dad to do that?

Absolutely nothing.

Nothing at all, Jotham.

And I've got Dad crying down the phone every night saying bring our boy back, wondering what they did wrong.

I said maybe we should have seen *Billy Elliot*, but Mum said that was too on the nose, so we went with the singing monkeys, and we were allowed a glass of Prosecco with our dough balls and we said cheers and, by the way, it was way more than I got when I passed my driving test.

We were so proud of you, Jotham.

You don't belong here.

None of you do.

Adira Do you want me to help you pack? We'll still get the train.

Tana I'm so sorry your mum said that to you, Adira. I'm so sorry. If you need to stay with us, you can share my bedroom anytime you like.

But for Jotham to say what he said.

When it did actually happen to you.

Jotham, that's –

I wish you could have our mum, Adira.

And our dad.

Adira Thanks.

I don't.

My mum's amazing.

Jen How can you say that?

Adira If you met her.

Jen Yeah but she told you she /

Adira I know.

And yeah, it was the worst thing ever.

But I'm still here.

In stupid Dungeness, on the edge of the bloody country. Are we even on the map? All I can see is the sea, there's never any signal and now there's no wifi thanks to you lot and I just want to look at my Snapchat /

Jotham   No one's messaged you, babes.

Adira   And send a message on Whatsapp and no one here looks like me. I see them staring at me, you all know they do.

Caia   They stare at us too, when I hold Franny's hand.

Adira   That's different.

And social services sent me out here to keep myself safe but I don't feel safer.

You don't know what I did to try and change this. For this not to be me. I prayed, so hard, so so hard, and, yeah, all along I thought this would be easier for everyone if I was dead.

So I go back and I say to them, *you* change. This is on you. You won't pray the gay away, you won't change our family's reputation, it won't do anything.

I'm gonna do the two minutes' silence. In the taxi or on the platform, I don't care, wherever I am, I'll do it. And I will pray for the victims and their families.

And I'm gonna pray for the strength to forgive my mum.

And I want to be there to help her. Because I need her to help me.

And one day, I think she will.

I still think you're all twats, though.

Jotham   But you'll add us on Facebook?

Adira   Of course.

It was me who put the bin in Jotham's bed.

Jotham   I knew it!

Adira   There's a limit to how many times we can hear 'Let It Go', Jotham.

I prayed for patience. But you sing it a lot.

Forgive me?

Jotham   Of course I forgive you, babes.

I was gonna make you a fierce outfit for Bournemouth Pride.

Shall I send it to you?

Adira   Why don't you bring it up to me one day?

What's so good about Bournemouth Pride anyway?

Jotham   Is she on glue?

Is this girl on glue?

What is so good about Bournemouth Pride?

Do you know where that yellow brick road leads?

Bournemouth Pride, that's where, babes.

Do you know what's at the end of the rainbow, Adira?

Bournemouth Pride, that's what.

And I swear I am going to be crowned queen of Bournemouth Pride and I'm gonna lead the parade on the winner's float, I'm gonna sit on my throne with my crown and drive through the streets of Bournemouth serving fuck-you realness and I'm gonna look so sickening, you lot are gonna gag, hunties.

And all the haters, I'm gonna make them eat it.

OK?

Caia   Yes, queen!

Orson   He'll put a dress on and drive through
Bournemouth pulled by a tractor but he won't stand out in
the street and protest in his jeans and t-shirt.

What have you got to say to that, Jotham?

Tana   Leave my brother alone.

Orson   Your brother's a hypocrite.

Jotham   No more than you.

Tana   My brother is amazing actually.

And at least he's not a bully.

So it's none of your business what he does.

Orson   Come on, Jotham, what have you got to say?

Jotham   Obviously it's sad and everything, and I don't
mean to be shallow, but can I have Adira's bedroom please?

Orson   Typical. Such a pageant queen. Being fabulous
doesn't make you safe.

Jotham   It does for me.

Orson   I don't want to be fabulous.

Jotham   There's no danger there, babes.

Orson   But it's a mask. What happens when you take it off?

Caia   Stop, no stop, I can't go on no please don't look at
me, don't look at me. Oh the pain.

Jen   Was it not about you for five seconds?

Birdie   Sorry, Adira, your moment's over.

Adira   Fine by me.

Caia   I have dreams.

Vast, open dreams.

Don't you?

Jotham   Who?

Caia   All of you?

Jotham   All of us what?

Caia   Have dreams?

Jotham   I'm still a virgin, so it's just the one dream at the moment.

Orson   You don't want it enough, Jotham, that's your problem.

Jotham   I do really want it.

Orson   The only person standing between you and your virginity is *you*.

Jotham   Well, no, you need another person really don't you?

Caia   Not to dream, Jotham. You don't need another person to dream.

Adira   I'm gonna get my bag.

Tana   Jotham, I'm gonna pack you a bag.

Start saying your goodbyes?

Jotham   You can't make me.

Adira   Tana, I'll help you.

Exit **Adira** *and* **Tana**.

Caia   Franny. Why?

Why are you torturing me like this?

Birdie   You're sixteen. I think you need to calm down a bit.

Caia   I can't make you love me, Franny, I know that. Oh Franny, beautiful, elegant and strange creature that you are, so out of context in this shitty house in Dungeness, England, I say to you this:

I love you. I absolutely fucking love you.

Franny –

Caia   FRANNY! I have Mc-fallen for you.

Enter **Adira** *and* **Tana** *with their bags.*

Adira   Is Ronald McDonald dead?

Orson   No, just in love.

Come on, Franny, give her a break.

Caia   I'll take lectures in love from anyone except you.

Orson   I've never given anyone lectures, thank you very much.

Caia   What do you know anyway, you have to fake a boyfriend.

Orson   He's real.

Caia   All your talk of love in the open, where is he then?

Orson   We don't kiss in the shadows any more than you do.

It's private that's all.

Caia   You're a hypocrite.

Adria   It's time to go.

Birdie   I can't make you stay, but I need to tell your social worker where you are.

Adira   I texted him.

Birdie   I'm sorry to see you go.

We love you and you'll always be welcome.

I hope your time at Spectrum was helpful.

Adira   Not really.

But thanks for being nice.

I'll send my brothers down for the rest of my stuff.

Birdie   Here's an evaluation form.

Or you can do it online.

Or you know, don't.

Adira *hugs everyone goodbye.*

She gets to **Jen** *last.*

Adira   See you, Jen.

Jen   –

Birdie   Is there anything you want to say to Adira, Jen?

Jen   –

Adira   Well, goodbye.

We're cool. Just so you know. It's all good.

We're gonna miss the train.

Jotham   I'm not coming, Tana.

Tana   I know.

Jotham   You'll come back down though?

Tana   Maybe.

Dunno.

You could come up for the weekend?

Jotham   Yeah.

Maybe.

Tana   You're my best brother.

I'm sorry I called you all freaks. You're not.

You're my best. OK?

Bye, Jotham.

Jotham   Bye.

Adira OK, so see you, I guess.

Tana *and* **Adira** *make their way to the door with their bags.*

Jotham I really miss Mum and Dad, Tana.

And you.

Especially you.

Tana OK.

Jotham Will you tell them I miss them?

A moment.

Tana No.

Come on, Adira.

Exit **Tana** *and* **Adira**.

Jen They're dropping like flies.

Caia You should have told her.

Jen Told her what?

Caia You're like a stone, I can't bear it, Jen.

Jen Yeah? Well at least I'm not on the floor dressed as Ronald McDonald.

Caia I don't care.

I don't care.

I'm sixteen, OK, so obviously that means I don't know shit.

But if life has taught me something, it's to be kind. And if you find someone that loves you, it's good. It's really good, Jen.

Jen I don't love her.

Caia Falling in love is very hard. Believe me. It's very hard.

But pretending you *haven't* fallen in love is even harder.

Birdie   OK, this is good. This is really good.

Jen, Jen, look at you, all connected and listening.

Jen   Shut up.

She's not gonna call me, is she, Birdie?

Birdie   Are you OK?

Jen   She's gone; you're kicking me out. I'm not having a very good day actually.

Birdie   Can we make a deal?

Jen   About what?

Birdie   What you said to Adira was wrong. And if you can't see that, I want to help you get to a point where you can.

And if I'm gonna do that, I'll need you to stick around. And, you know, we'd miss you.

So can we make a deal? If you want to, you can stay, but there's a condition.

You stop throwing stones at our window please.

Jen *thinks.*

Eventually she empties some pebbles from her pockets and gives them to **Birdie**.

Birdie   Thank you.

Thank you.

Did you see that, Orson? It's what, in the trade, we call a breakthrough moment.

BOOM-CHICKA-ROCKA-SUCK-ON-THAT.

Right. We've got to make up our minds.

Inside or outside?

Together or separate?

Orson Don't give them the choice.

Jotham I don't want to do it outside.

Orson I think you'll regret it.

Jotham I know what happened was awful and I want to say that. But I don't know how because doing it outside it's /

Orson It's the only way. You want to show your anger and solidarity, it counts for nothing unless people see it.

Birdie Don't pressurise him.

Orson Someone's got to.

Caia I'm going outside and I'm taking my Franny's hand /

Orson There we go.

That's what I'm talking about.

Birdie Orson, stop it.

You're not in charge.

Orson Well, you certainly aren't either.

What kind of outfit do you call this?

You've got two that just left right under your nose, you've got one who thinks she's Ronald McDonald and one who's smashing the place in every time we go to bed.

Birdie You're part of the same group.

Orson I'm at least a year older than everyone here.

At least.

Birdie Except me.

Jotham So, what, that makes you better?

Orson It makes me more mature.

Jen It makes you a dickhead.

Orson You're all cowards.

You make me sick the lot of you.

Birdie   Oi, that's enough.

Jotham   I'm not doing the silence with him.

Jen   Or me.

Orson   We all do it together.

Birdie   Why?

Orson   I can't believe you need that explaining.

Caia   Orson, stop being so unkind.

Orson   Oh shut up, Ronald McDonald, go get me a Big Mac.

Caia   Hey.

Birdie   That's not helpful.

Orson   Oh get back in your closet.

Birdie   It's a multi-purpose room.

Jotham   We're running out of time.

Orson   Why don't you put your dress on, princess?

Jotham   Oh you'd like that would you?

Orson   Birdie, get it together.

Caia   She's got it together . . .

Jotham   Stop bullying us, Orson.

Orson   You think you're being bullied, look how the world treats you.

Birdie   Everyone please calm down.

Orson   Go get fingered then dumped again.

Birdie   She broke my heart, Orson.

Orson   I'm going outside, who's coming?

Jotham   I want to stay here.

Orson   Nice bit of pride you got going on, princess.

Jotham   I am proud.

Orson   No you're not.

Birdie   What do you know?

Caia   Ronald McDonald says –

Jotham   Fuck off, Ronald. You look like a joke.

Caia   You fuck off.

Birdie   We haven't got time for this.

Orson   Everyone out together.

Jotham   You are not in charge.

Orson   Nor are you.

Birdie   I'm in charge.

Orson   Good one, Birdie.

Birdie   I swear to God, I'm gonna kill you.

Jotham   Get him, Birdie.

Caia   Stop it, you lot.

Jotham   I'll get you, my pretty, and your little dog too.

Orson   I don't have a dog.

Birdie   Shut up, Orson.

Orson   Who's got a dog?

Jotham   Fly, my pretties.

Orson   Not so big now are you?

Jotham   I am big. It's Bournemouth Pride that got small.

Orson   He's speaking in tongues.

Jotham   You're a shit gay, Orson.

Orson   *You're* a shit gay.

Jotham   I am a great gay.

Orson   You're a great gay bellend.

And you, Birdie.

Birdie   What about me?

Orson   Call yourself a lesbian?

My mum's a bigger lesbian than you.

Birdie   I'm not surprised. Have you seen your dad?

Orson   I'm gonna kill you.

Birdie   Not if I kill you first.

Jotham   Stella!

Orson   Who the fuck is Stella?

Birdie   Come on, Orson, I swear to God you are so done.

Orson   Yeah?

Etc.

The argument descends into an enormous ad lib argument.

It gets louder and louder and more vicious until everyone is stood up screaming in each other's faces. When we think it can't get any worse . . .

Franny   HEY!

STOP IT

ALL OF YOU.

I SAID, STOP IT.

Silence.

Caia   Franny!

You're alive.

It's a miracle.

Enter **Adira** *and* **Tana**.

Adira There's all these people in the streets, we couldn't get a taxi.

Tana We knew we were gonna miss the train so we came back.

What's going on?

Caia Franny has come back to us, that's what's happened.

Franny I'll tell you what's going on.

Orson. You're a real wanker sometimes.

Birdie is trying.

She is trying so hard.

And you lot. You smug, entitled idiots.

You think someone blowing you up is the biggest thing you've got to worry about?

You're doing a good enough job of that on your own.

What do you want? What do you *actually want*?

When we walk down the streets holding hands, we're making a statement. When we kiss at the bus stop or at the movies, we're making a statement.

And love starts where the movies end. It's scary, cos you have to show someone the bits of you you don't even show yourself, but lots of things in life are scary and you still do it.

I know you lot don't like Orson. I get it. I don't like him much either. But he's found someone and if that's what he wants in life then leave him alone.

And Orson, Birdie is trying. Give her a break.

Jotham doesn't have to go outside, and Jen, Adira doesn't have to love you back if she can't. You can't make her. But you fell in love, you should be happy that you can, because if you can now, you will again, and one time that person will love you back and it will be amazing and wonderful and you'll never be the same again because you were brave enough to let someone love you and that's what's at the end of the rainbow.

Jotham   No, it is actually Bournemouth Pride.

Franny   So I ask you again. All of you.

What do you actually want?

Jotham   I think I preferred her when she wasn't speaking.

Birdie   I know what I want.

I can tell you exactly what I want.

All these haters out there. They're nothing.

All you lot, saying you hate me, even though I'm trying, I'm really trying. Doesn't mean a thing.

Believe me. No can hate me more than I do sometimes.

Franny   But what do you want?

Birdie   What I want is to look at myself in the mirror and maybe one day, just one out of the seven, for me to look in the mirror and like what I see. Just one day out of seven to look at myself and say, 'Today, I'm enough'.

And I can. I can do it.

I don't know where I learned to hate myself so much, but I will be damned if I'm gonna let it get in my way.

That's what I want.

Because today, I'm enough.

Caia   I know what I want.

Franny, I know I've been a bit over the top, looking back I can see how this might have all come across as a bit, I don't know, desperate or something.

But I love you. And I want you as my wife. And if one day, you then become my husband, I want that too.

Franny, please.

Will you marry me?

Franny –

Jotham's *alarm goes off.*

Jotham   It's time.

Caia   Franny?

Birdie   Everyone ready?

Caia   Franny?

Birdie   Caia, you'll have to wait.

Orson   But we haven't decided.

Birdie   We'll have to do it just as we are.

Take us as they find us, right?

Jotham   It's time.

Birdie   OK. Ready everyone?

Jotham   I'm ready.

Adira   We're all ready.

House lights up slowly through the following.

Birdie   We will all now observe two minutes' silence.

Stand if you wish, or stay seated, but I ask all of us to honour this moment.

For all those living in fear, far from us, or on our doorstep, we show you our solidarity; for all those fighting for their right to love, to be themselves in all corners of the world, for all those who have fought before us. For everyone who has fought in the name of love.

We stand in solidarity and we remember them now. And we say, *love wins*.

Two minutes' silence.

We begin now.

We observe two minutes' silence.

After the silence.

From outside we can hear a choir sing a song we know.

Through the frosted window we get the sense of a crowd congregating. We see the blurred shapes of rainbow flags drifting by. More and more people are walking by the window.

The song gets louder and louder through the following.

Birdie   Thank you, everyone.

Caia   Franny?

Jen   What's all that noise?

Jotham   It sounds like an army.

Birdie   Let's go see.

Exit **Birdie**, **Orson**, **Tana** *and* **Jotham**.

Now the whole crowd is singing along.

Franny   Caia.

I love you too.

But of course I'm not gonna marry you.

I'm sixteen.

Enter **Jotham**.

Jotham   Guys, you've got to come see this.

Guys, come on.

Caia, Franny, Adira, come on.

Jen.

They're all headed to the beach, Jen.

There's flags and banners and candles and lanterns and the sun is shining and /

Caia.

Franny.

Hurry up, you'll miss it.

Jen.

Adira.

Come on!

Come with me!

Come outside.

It's beautiful.

Adira, **Jen**, **Caia** *and* **Franny** *follow* **Jotham** *onto the street.*

We're outside now.

They join a huge throng of people with flags and banners who have taken to the streets singing the song we all know.

The rousing song builds and builds. They stand downstage taking it all in.

They sing.

We sing.

The powerful, uplifting climax of the song and a triumph of rainbow flags.

Blackout.

Printed in the USA
CPSIA information can be obtained
at www.ICGtesting.com
LVHW020935171024
794056LV00003B/772